EXTREME BOARD Makeover

MICHAEL L. STICKLER
with ARTHUR W. RITTER

THE Vision GROUP LTD

Extreme Board Makeover
Author Mike Stickler *with* Arthur W. Ritter

Printed in the United States of America

ISBN 978-0-9907441-7-7

THE VISION GROUP LTD

The Vision Group, Ltd., TheVisionGroupLtd.com
MikeStickler.online

EXTREME BOARD *Makeover*
TABLE OF CONTENTS

Welcome and Introduction 3

Why Do I Need a Board? 5

Board Models 6
    The Elder Model
    The "I Don't Want to Lose Control" Model
    The Secular Model
    The Ideal Model
Discussion: What Model is Your Leadership Board Employing?...............8
Board Responsibilities 9
Board vs. Staff Responsibilities 18

Who's on Board..19
Board Composition Analysis Tool 20
People to Have on a Leadership Board 23
Recruiting Board Members..24
You're on the Board: Now What? 28
Suggestions For a Board Orientation Program 29
Ongoing Board Training 30

Role of the Board Officers 31
Role of the Board Chairperson...33
Board Committees 34
Activity: Committee Terms of Reference 37
Conclusion..40
Resources 41

WELCOME

Considering the demands placed on individuals today, we appreciate you taking the time to work through what we certainly hope will be an eye-opening and potential-unlocking workbook. We're here to teach you concepts and principles you can use in any ministry for the rest of your life.

The Vision Group, Ltd., (TVG) has put together a team of staff members who each have more than a decade of experience working with faith-based ministries. We've seen wonderful ministries thrive and grow, but we've also seen them die on the vine simply because of a lack of steady support. For this reason, we've joined forces to provide faith-based nonprofits with a professional, focused and proven business resource.

WE WANT TO SEE FULLY FUNDED, FAITH-BASED MINISTRIES FULFILLING THEIR CALL TO SERVE GOD'S PEOPLE WORLDWIDE.

TVG is dedicated to connecting God's people with the resources needed to build strong foundations and realize their dreams. We want to help you address financial issues and create a plan to ensure the long-term health and viability of your ministry. Doing so frees you to refocus on your calling and enjoy the peace of mind that comes with good stewardship.

Within this workbook, we plan to broaden your understanding of ministry boards, including various board models, board member responsibilities, recruitment, orientation and much, much more. By the end of this workbook, you will truly know what it takes to have the "most effective leadership board on the planet." We look forward to your knowledge increasing as we share ideas and explore these new concepts together.

WHY DO I NEED A BOARD?

Nonprofit ministries receive billions of dollars each year in public money. This money takes many forms, including government grants and donations from companies, foundations and private individuals. In fact, more than 70 percent of all money going to nonprofit groups in the U.S. comes from private individuals just like you. Because ministries are entrusted with so much public money, U.S. law requires that each nonprofit organization establish a board of directors (sometimes called a church council or elder board) to ensure good stewardship of the money donated to it.

Think of your leadership board as the owners of a company. Like owners of a company, board members govern the organization, carry out fiscal responsibilities and determine policies that guide and support the organization. However, unlike the owners of a company, board members are volunteers. They serve without salaries, and they don't benefit financially from the organization. Because board members don't receive a salary or share of the profits, they can put the needs of the ministry first.

BOARD MODELS

There are no set requirements for how to set up a nonprofit board. Some ministries have three board members, while others have 30. The minimum number of board members your ministry must have is typically spelled out in your bylaws and is governed by state law. Most states require at least three board members, while others require at least two. According to a survey by the group BoardSource, the average size of a board is 19 members. Overall, organizations with larger budgets tend to have larger boards.

When it comes to board structure and size, there are a number of different models out there. We've lumped them into four types: the Elder Model, the "I Don't Want to Lose Control" Model, the Secular Nonprofit Model, and, finally, what we consider to be the Ideal Model.

- The Elder Model: Boards that rely on the Elder Model are typically composed of influential lay leaders who are likely involved because of their financial or ministerial influence. In this model, board members provide feedback and counsel to the senior leadership in the church and work very closely with the leadership. These boards are typically small – composed of five people or so – and they may be overworked because of their small size. They often don't have the breadth of skills and experience required to support the ministry's mission.

- The "I Don't Want to Lose Control" Model: In this model, the visionary/founder of the ministry sits on the board and essentially runs both the board and the ministry herself. The board members are simply figureheads and "yes" men. They don't have in-depth information about the organization and therefore cannot provide sound counsel. Fiscal controls are generally not in place.

- The Secular Model: The Secular Nonprofit Model employs a large, all-volunteer board where members operate at different levels of participation. Some members may be deeply involved, as with the Elder Model, while others are merely figureheads, as with the "I Don't Want to Lose Control" Model. Despite this diversity in levels of commitment, all board members have an equal vote, and all authority rests in them. This type of board also may not see the visionary/founder as an integral part of the ministry, leading to tension among board members. And decision-making may be difficult because of the number of board members who are permitted to offer opinions on board decisions.

The Ideal Model: What we see as the Ideal Model is in reality a hybrid model. The founder/visionary is not a board member, but instead is a paid staff person. The board has two levels of participation and authority. There is an inner circle of close advisors that really understands and supports the visionary/founder. We call this the Executive Committee, and it closely resembles an elder board. This group may be composed of five or so people. This group makes recommendations to the board-at-large for a "yea" or "nay" vote. The board-at-large is a much larger group – up to 25 people – who are less informed and less involved, but may have money or important community connections. This group accepts or rejects recommendations it receives from that Executive Committee.

There are many benefits to this model. First, the visionary/founder receives a high level of support from the board. Second, the board is large enough that board members represent a variety of skills and have numerous contacts in the community that can be tapped on behalf of the ministry. Third, the Executive Committee structure ensures quick decision-making despite the board's size. And finally, the board-at-large serves as a training ground for developing new leadership that could, in time, be added to the Executive Committee, preventing burn out of Executive Committee members.

DISCUSSION:
WHAT MODEL IS YOUR
LEADERSHIP BOARD EMPLOYING?

How many people are on the board?

Who are they; what are their skills and experience?

Is the Executive Director on the board?

How are they selected?

How are decisions made?

Are financial controls in place?

BOARD RESPONSIBILITIES

Let's look more closely at the responsibilities of the Board of Directors. We can break down board responsibilities into four categories, each of which we will look at in turn:

1. Planning or setting the overall direction of the organization

2. Ensuring sufficient human resources are in place

3. Overseeing the financial health of the organization including fundraising

4. Making sure all legal expectations are met

1. SETTING DIRECTION

Board members serve as captains of the ship, setting a course for the ministry they govern. As part of their responsibility as captains of the ship, board members may develop or review the organization's mission and vision statements; determine strategic direction, goals, outcomes, and action plans; continually review community needs and trends; and evaluate programs.

If you've attended our "Grant-Writing and Fundraising for Christian Ministries" seminar, you've heard us talk about the importance of defining your MVVG – your mission, vision, values and goals. This is a key job for your board, and something board members should review annually.

Let's face it, organizations can't be all things to all people. In fact, a focused organization is a more effective organization. Clearly defining your church or ministry will help you better assess opportunities for program expansion and fundraising.

VISION

First, let's focus on the broadest way to define your organization – your vision. Your vision is the greatest accomplishment you can imagine. For example, the vision of The Vision Group, Ltd. is "envision Christian ministries, churches and community nonprofit organizations, and those who give to their support, fulfilling their missions to serve people worldwide and advance the Kingdom of God." Your vision shapes everything that you do. Another ministry's vision may be "to end homelessness." Notice these vision statements are short, only one sentence long, action-oriented and easy to remember.

If a ministry ever becomes confused, board members and staff could ask themselves, "Will this help us achieve the vision?" Vision helps provide clarity and is invaluable in recruiting supporters. A strong vision sells itself.

MISSION

While your vision is the grandest accomplishment you can imagine, your mission tells people how you carry out that vision. Your mission describes your style, technique or method you use to achieve your vision.

At The Vision Group, Ltd., our mission is to connect God's people with the resources needed to build strong foundations and realize their dreams. As you'll notice, it is specific enough to give people an idea of the methods we use, but broad enough to allow us to grow within our vision.

One of our clients has the following vision and mission statements: the vision is to empower parents so they can change the unwanted behaviors of their children. The organization does this through its mission, which is to provide troubled families a vehicle for developing the habits and attributes of loving, responsible, self-controlled lifestyles and relationships. Think of it this way: your vision states your dream, while your mission tells people how you will achieve it.

VALUES

Your values help define what is important and acceptable to you. They help keep you on the straight and narrow. To use a driving analogy, your values are the guardrails of life.

At The Vision Group, Ltd., our values are "faith, hope and love." This means that everything we say and do should convey or support faith in God, hope for the future and love for ourselves and others. If we find these three values missing from something we've said and done, it's time to make a correction.

GOALS

Goals are specific benchmarks you wish to achieve. A good goal has:

- A clearly defined objective
- Action steps
- A timeline

In addition, goals must be capable of being written down and shared with others, from staff members to volunteers to foundations. For example, a poorly formed goal would be "to help poor kids be safe, healthy and happy." There's no way to measure when you've achieved that goal.

Here's a better goal: "We will improve literacy rates among low-income youth in Reno. We will do this by elevating reading scores by 50 percent among third and fourth graders through a weekly mentoring program at Washoe Elementary School during the 20XX-20XX school year." That's a measurable goal. You know when you've achieved success.

One last thought: Entire books are written about mission, vision, values and goals. It takes some time and effort to go through the process, but it is well worth it. Be patient, and let the Holy Spirit guide you. Remember, this is a valuable part of your board work.

SWOT ANALYSIS

When engaging in traditional strategic planning, debating future direction or assessing existing opportunities, boards often rely on a SWOT analysis, a technique that comes from the business world. SWOT stands for strengths, weaknesses, opportunities and threats. In conducting a SWOT analysis, the board lists and assesses the organization's strengths, weaknesses, opportunities, and threats. Each of these controlling forces prompts the board to consider factors that might easily be overlooked as it shapes the future of the organization.

This process provides insight into the organization's internal and external positioning by examining internal and external elements that must be factored into future decision making. It prohibits the organization from becoming too insular and functioning without proper feedback.

For example, your organization has run a successful after school program for a number of years and is now considering a preschool. Your SWOT analysis might look something like this:

Strengths: Working with children Own large facility already	Weaknesses: Limited staff without teaching credentials Lack of awareness in the community
Opportunities: Local church closed its preschool last year Parents are asking if we will provide preschool	Threats: Private group wants to open preschool in our area

Likely your SWOT analysis would be much more extensive, with many factors listed under each heading. The key is to write down every piece of information that might factor into your decision making. You might try this on a large whiteboard or chalkboard. Or, you can even use a blank wall and post-it notes. The key is to ensure that everyone can see the items listed under each heading.

2. HUMAN RESOURCES

Members of the board must ensure the nonprofit organization has adequate human resources in place. This includes a number of aspects. For example, board members hire, evaluate and, when necessary, terminate the chief executive of the ministry (commonly called the Executive Director). This means board members must define the qualities and experience necessary for a chief executive, develop a job description and establish a salary. Most small ministries already have a visionary/founder ready to assume the role of chief executive, but if not, the board must conduct a search for an appropriate chief executive who meets the established requirements.

Once the chief executive is in place, the board must provide support to help her achieve the organization's mission. This is one of the reasons we feel so strongly about a two-tiered board structure, with a small Executive Committee that can provide extensive moral support. That same Executive Committee should evaluate the performance of the chief executive on an annual basis.

According to a National Center for Nonprofit Boards and Stanford University study, 84 percent of nonprofits reported that their boards conduct an annual evaluation of their chief executive. For the most part, the study found, the Executive Committee conducts the evaluation (47 percent), although the board chair, a committee or the entire board sometimes conducts the evaluation.

Let's face it, being evaluated may sound a little intimidating. But the process has some clear benefits for both the Executive Director and the board. In order for the evaluation to occur, the Executive Director must have a clear job description that outlines his responsibility and authority. He must also have clear goals and expectations for each year. This helps provide a framework for each year's work and ensures the mission is being met. Evaluations also provide a time for the Executive Director and the board to discuss any budding disagreements or concerns. Hopefully you are discussing these all year long, but if not, evaluation time provides the perfect opportunity. This ensures there are no surprise departures of the Executive Director.

We'll just briefly touch on the board's other responsibilities when it comes to human resources. The board is responsible for approving the creation of additional staff positions. The board also develops human resource policies and procedures and ensures fair and ethical treatment of staff and volunteers. Finally, the board monitors and resolves any conflicts of interest, which we will discuss in detail later in this seminar.

3. FINANCIAL HEALTH

Next, the board oversees the financial health of the organization. Board members approve an annual operating budget and ensure that adequate financial controls are in place. These controls include segregating financial duties; protecting cash receipts; requiring second signatures on large checks; keeping track of inventory, including expensive equipment like computers and copiers; ensuring a fair and efficient bidding process for contracts; producing timely financial reports; and maintaining accurate record keeping. Many ministries use QuickBooks or QuickBooks for Nonprofits to help with reporting and record keeping. Using an accounting package (rather than a checkbook or spreadsheet) helps board members easily track income and expenses against the budget plan and aids in the preparation of year-end financial statements and tax forms.

According to *Financial Responsibilities of Nonprofit Boards,* there are ten key financial questions that board members should ask (and know the answer to). They are:

- Have we run a gain or loss? (i.e., are we better or worse off financially than we were a year ago?)

- Are our key sources of income rising or falling? If they are falling, what can be done to change that?

- Are our key expenses, especially salary and benefits, under control?

- Do we have sufficient reserves?

- Has the board adopted a formal policy for the establishment of reserves? Is our cash flow projected to be adequate?

- Are we regularly comparing our financial activity with what we have budgeted?

- Is our financial plan consistent with our strategic plan?

- Is our staff satisfied and productive?

- Are we filing, on a timely basis, all the reporting documents we are supposed to be filing?

- Are we fulfilling all of our legal obligations?

FUNDRAISING

The second, and perhaps even more important, element of financial health is that the leadership board must plan for and assist with acquiring sufficient resources to operate the organization effectively. In short, think of the board as your primary fundraising team. This responsibility has two parts:

- Each board member must commit to making a sacrificial contribution of their time, talent and treasures, and
- Each board member must share their community of relationships and engage in fundraising.

Let's look at each of these responsibilities individually. First, each board member must make a sacrificial gift. Think about it this way. We all have pocket money. For most of us, pocket money is the $20 bills we get out of the ATM. But for a billionaire, pocket money might be $20,000. Pocket money is the money you can give away without batting an eye. It's different for different people. In contrast, a sacrificial gift is a gift that is significant to the person offering up the gift. Sacrificial giving may require careful consideration and prayer. It's a leap of faith. Again, the amount that qualifies as a sacrifice will be different for an elderly woman on a fixed income versus the CEO of Microsoft.

Now you may be asking yourself, "Why is making a sacrificial gift so important?" Because a board member cannot, in good faith, encourage others to support an organization she is not herself supporting. Imagine a church council member who is asking a church member to commit to the capital campaign. The church member asks, "Well, have you and your family made a commitment to the campaign?" If the council member's response is "no," the church member will think, "If the church council isn't behind it, why should I be?" But imagine if the church council member can explain how she put off buying a new car so she could make a contribution to the campaign. That's sacrificial giving, and it has a powerful effect on others!

That brings us to the second part of the board's fundraising responsibility: board members must harness their community of relationships, engage in fundraising and support the ministry. Board members have to be willing to open up their networks and make connections. Perhaps one board member could introduce you to the mayor. Another might know a staff person at a local foundation. Your board members need to be willing to make these introductions on your organization's behalf. After all, these are your primary partners.

4. LEGAL AND ETHICAL EXPECTATIONS

Finally, the board must ensure all legal and ethical expectations are met. For incorporated organizations, this includes maintaining a list of names and addresses of board members as well as a minute book with minutes from all board meetings. If the nonprofit organization is incorporated, the board must make sure it complies with reporting requirements, including producing financial statements, filing tax documents, and registering annually with the state if required.

The board also is required to ensure the organization is run according to its established Constitution (or Articles of Incorporation, if incorporated) and bylaws, and to update the bylaws as often as necessary.

Think of the Constitution (or Articles of Incorporation) as a legal description of the "what" of your organization. In general, your organization's Constitution will include such information as your organization's legal name, location of its head office, whether or not it is affiliated with, or part of, another organization (e.g., a local chapter of a national association), number of members (if there is a limit on your membership numbers), and a description of your board and Executive Committee (number of directors, names of table officer positions).

The bylaws are a legal description of the "how" of your organization. They are "operating instructions" that can clarify as well as limit the board's authority in an organization, and empower members to hold the board accountable for its decisions. Bylaws contain not only the number of board members required, but also instructions on how often the board must meet, where and how the board will meet, information on officers and how they are selected, committee structure and much more.

Aside from legal requirements, board members must ensure business is conducted according to ethical norms. A key element of maintaining high ethical standards is instituting a solid conflict of interest policy. Conflict of interest is when a board (or staff member) puts his personal or professional concerns ahead of the welfare of the ministry. Because board members often have many connections to businesses and other community groups, it is not unusual for potential conflicts of interest to occur.

For example, let's say your ministry is going to purchase a new copy machine. The organization has a policy that requires soliciting competitive bids on all equipment purchases over $5,000. One of your board members owns a business machines store and offers to give the ministry a good deal on a copier. The board decides to skip the competitive process and award the contract to the board member. This is clearly a conflict of interest.

The ministry would have been better served by going through the competitive bidding process. If the board member's business chose to submit a bid, the board member should have declared her association with the company and abstained from the selection process. If the board member's firm won the bid, she would need to abstain from all future board actions associated with the contract.

According to BoardSource, a good conflict of interest policy should contain the following elements:

1. FULL DISCLOSURE
Board members and staff members in decision-making roles should make known their connections with groups doing business with the organization. This information should be provided annually.

2. BOARD MEMBER ABSTENTION FROM DISCUSSION AND VOTING
Board members who have an actual or potential conflict of interest should not participate in discussions or vote on matters affecting transactions between the organization and the other group.

3. STAFF MEMBER ABSTENTION FROM DECISION-MAKING
Staff members who have an actual or potential conflict should not be substantively involved in decision-making affecting such transactions.

BOARD RESPONSIBILITIES
VERSUS
STAFF RESPONSIBILITIES

Many boards get tripped up when it comes to delineating their role in relation to the role of paid staff. A board member might not like the way a certain junior staff person (not the Executive Director) is performing his or her job. Should the board member address the issue with that staff person? Or the office copier breaks down, and the organization needs a new one. The funds aren't in the budget. Can the Executive Director go ahead and purchase the copier without board approval? These can be tricky situations.

In the first scenario, the organization's Executive Director is responsible for managing the junior staff on a day-to-day basis. The board does not supervise the staff with the exception of the Executive Director, so this situation should be left up to the Executive Director. In the second scenario, the board sets the annual budget and must approve any changes to it. Thus, the Executive Director can't buy the new copier until the board adds the funds to the budget.

Separating board and staff responsibilities is easier if you think about each group's focus. Broadly speaking, the board is responsible for overall planning and policy development, as well as approving and evaluating policies. The staff implements the policies and plans, broadly speaking. A worksheet differentiating board and staff responsibilities is included in the Appendix to help you clarify board and staff roles.

Although we suggest a strict delineation of board/staff duties, it is not unusual for staff members to be included in board activities. For example, the chief executive often collaborates with the board chairman on development of the board meeting agendas. Staff members may attend board meetings to give reports; for example, the Development Director may provide a progress report on a major grant application, and the Finance Director may provide financial reports. But it's important to note that staff members do not have a vote and do not offer opinions or engage in discussion unless asked by a board member. Finally, staff members may be members of board committees. For example, the Development Director would be a logical addition to the Finance or Fundraising Committee.

WHO'S ON BOARD?

Now that we've established the very important role the board of directors plays in your ministry, how do you know who should be on your board? To help you figure this out, let's first look at the basic requirements for the job of board member. These are:

- a sincere conviction that the organization performs a useful public service
- a concern with the organization's place in the overall community program
- a sense of financial responsibility for the wise spending of donated funds

Expanding upon these basic requirements, board members have duties that they must carry out under the law. These duties are care, loyalty and obedience. We touched on the duty of care earlier. Most standards call for the board members to use the same care "that an ordinarily prudent person would exercise in a like position under similar circumstances." Board members demonstrate care when they attend and participate regularly in board meetings, are objective and show independent judgment when voting, are well-informed, delegate only to trustworthy people and follow up regularly. The duty of loyalty means that the board member gives the highest priority to the "total" organization. The duty of obedience means board members ensure that the ministry remains obedient to the central purposes for which it was established. These are spelled out in the Articles of Incorporation.

So, first we must ensure all potential board candidates fit the three basic requirements and are fit to carry out the three basic duties. Second, we need to ensure we have a diverse board in terms of demographics and skills, abilities and areas of influence. This means we must:

- Analyze the current composition of the board
- Note where we have holes in terms of skills, abilities and demographics
- Prioritize the areas where we are lacking skills, abilities and influence
- Find new board members with the qualities we currently lack

To accomplish this task, we recommend using a Board Composition Analysis Tool. This tool allows you to review what each board member brings to the organization and to see "holes" that need to be filled.

BOARD COMPOSITION
ANALYSIS TOOLS

Procedure to Use Board Composition Analysis Tool:

To use the Board Composition Analysis Tool, follow the steps listed below:

- Across the top of the chart, write the names of all current board members.

- Assess the qualities each board member brings to the board. Move down the column, checking off whether or not the particular board member possesses each quality, e.g., are of influence, expertise, experience.

- When all the board members have been assessed, look at the completed chart as a whole. Identify areas in which expertise or influence is lacking, and prioritize those critical to the operation of your board. Assess whether the board's composition is representative by gender and by age group.

- Based on the under-represented factors and identified priorities, identify a list of qualities that new board members should possess in order to improve the board's composition. Use this list when identifying potential candidates for board membership.

You should note that the blank Board Composition Analysis Tool identifies general needs. The needs of your organization may differ from these. Adapt the tool to your own needs.

BOARD COMPOSITION ANALYSIS TOOL: PAGE 1

FACTORS	VARIABLES	TRUSTEE'S NAME	TRUSTEE'S NAME	TRUSTEE'S NAME
DEMO-GRAPHICS	Years on the board			
	Sex: Female			
	Male			
	Age: Over 65			
	51-65			
	36-50			
	21-35			
	Community Districts Represented			
EDUCATION	University Degree			
	Law			
	Accounting/ Economics/ Commerce			
	Arts/Science			
	Education			
	Other			
	Certificates/ Courses or Equivalent Experience			
	Volunteer Management			
	Fundraising			
	Marketing			
	Public Admin.			
	Board Development			
	Personal Admin.			

BOARD COMPOSITION ANALYSIS TOOL: PAGE 2

FACTORS	VARIABLES	TRUSTEE'S NAME	TRUSTEE'S NAME	TRUSTEE'S NAME
EXPERIENCE	Meeting Management			
	Supervisory			
	Public Policy			
	Management /Admin.			
	Research			
KNOWL-EDGE/ SKILLS	Framework Policies			
	Governance Policies			
	Financial Policies			
	Advocacy Policies			
	Program Policies			
	Legal Agreements			
	Financial Statements			
	Grant Submissions			
	Fundraising			
	Recruitment / Training & Orientation			
	Media Relations			
	Gov't Relations			
	Short - and Long - Term Planning			
	Strategic Planning			
AREAS OF INFLUENCE	Business & Industry			
	Civic Gov't			
	Other Nonprofit Organizations			
	Educations/ Institutions			
	Federal Gov't			
	Media			
	Provincial Gov't			

PEOPLE TO HAVE ON A LEADERSHIP BOARD

Let's talk about some valuable people to have on your initial leadership board. These people will bring valuable skills, experience and advice to board discussions. Don't expect to add them all at the beginning, but think about collecting these skills over time. They are:

CPA – CPAs are known for their utmost integrity. Having a CPA on the board not only provides credibility and accountability, but also ensures that bookkeeping is accurate. A CPA also might be able to assist with preparations for the annual audit and make recommendations for potential auditors.

Financial Advisor – This person could be a banker or an investment advisor. A financial advisor is critical to your leadership team because he has access to funding and may have connections with many wealthy people. He can also help major donors learn how donations can be a win-win situation both for the donor and for the ministry.

Graphic Designer – You never get a second chance to make a first impression. Graphic designers ensure your ministry makes a good first impression through logos, brochures, newsletters, the web and much more.

Lawyer – Legal minds are great for keeping you on the straight and narrow. They can help review documents, draft contracts and lend advice. Legal counsel also can help translate local laws and regulation, which often are written in "legalese."

Media Specialist – Perhaps this person is a journalist, radio personality, producer or public relations specialist. Any way you look at it, a media savvy board member can help you bring your ministry's message to a wider audience. They may be invaluable at drafting press releases, getting media to your special events and placing stories on radio, TV and the local news. This skill set is critical since raising awareness often precedes raising funds.

Pastor – A pastor lends spiritual maturity to your board and ensures the ministry stays biblical when it might have a tendency to drift. Pastors can offer wise counsel and are often well connected in the community. They can also lend the strength of their congregation to your ministry.

Printer – We've talked about the importance of making a good first impression through brochures, newsletters and other printed material. A printer can help you produce these items for free or very low cost. Printers also are typically involved with so many local businesses that they "know everyone." They would be a valuable addition to your team.

High Profile Community Leader – This person could be the former mayor or another elected official willing to offer his or her name to your cause. This can add visibility, credibility and star power to your ministry. Be careful, though, especially if you are tapping an elected official. Elected officials are rarely brought into office with 100 percent of the voters in favor of him or her. Sometimes a more distant figure – like a senator – may be less controversial than the mayor, who is in the news on a daily basis. Retired leaders also can be less controversial figures.

Expert in Your Ministry's Field – Boards lend credibility to a ministry's work. If you are running a clinic in Africa, you might want to add a medical doctor to your board. If your ministry operates a recovery program, you might add a licensed alcohol and drug counselor. Experts not only add credibility, but can also help you implement best practices in your field.

These suggestions are just that – suggestions. Always remember to trust the Lord to give you the right people to lead your ministry.

RECRUITING BOARD MEMBERS

When looking for new board members, think through the people you have relationships with. Invite them to learn more about your ministry by touring your facility or experiencing your program. Share your vision for the ministry. If they catch it, they might be a good addition to your team.

Once you have your core group together, you might look among friends and acquaintances of current and former board members, staff, volunteers, donors and clients. Each prospective board member should receive a letter inviting them to consider board membership, as well as a personal visit from one or two board members to discuss the invitation and what it means. Make sure the candidate has an opportunity to ask questions about board structure, responsibilities and relationship with staff, as well as the ministry's programs, constituents and financial status. The prospective board member should receive key background materials that will help with insight into the workings of the board, including:

- An annual report (if available)

- The most recent year-end financial statement

- The strategic plan

- A list of current board members, titles and all affiliations

- A description of board members' responsibilities

- A board organization chart

- A staff organization chart

- The ministry's newsletter, brochure or other publications

- Recent newspaper or magazine articles about the ministry

Then, allow the candidate to sit in on a couple of board meetings. This allows him to see how the meetings are run and to meet all fellow board members. If he agrees to be nominated to serve on the board, have him complete a Nominating Form, which discusses his work history, community involvement and volunteer experience and how he can contribute to the board. This Nominating Form will be brought to the full board for review prior to the meeting approving new board members.

NOMINATION FORM: BOARD OF DIRECTORS

I, _____

On behalf of _____

Nominate: _____

For the election to the Board of Directors of _____

Date: _____ Signature: _____

I, _____
Accept the nomination.

Date: _____ Signature: _____

Position: _____

Address: _____

City: _____ Postal Code: _____

Telephone: (W) _____ (H): _____

Work History: Briefly describe your work experience (your last two-three jobs), in terms of the position held, the organization you worked for and your responsibilities:

_____

_____

_____

_____

_____

_____

_____

Community Involvement: Briefly describe your experience as a participant/member in activities e.g., Committees, Programs, Events, etc.

_____

_____

_____

_____

_____

_____

_____

Volunteer Experience: Briefly describe your volunteer experience, e.g., have you sat on other Boards of Directors, Committees, etc.?

_____

_____

_____

_____

_____

_____

Work Area: Each board member will take responsibility for an area of work. Please indicate the area of most interest to you according to your skills and interests.

_____	Finances
_____	Program Planning
_____	Human Resources
_____	Revenue Generation
_____	Building/Maintenance
_____	Special Events
_____	Marketing/Public Relations
_____	Other, specify: _____

Specific Skills: (Financial Management, Publicity & Marketing, Arts, Policy Development, Education & Training, Media & Public Relations, Human Resources, Legal Support, Internet/Web, Others)

_____

_____

_____

_____

_____

_____

Candidate's Declaration:

I, _____, support the vision and mission statement of

_____.

Date: _____ Signature: _____

Adding a new member to the leadership team is not something to be taken lightly by either the prospective new member or the existing leadership board. Prospective board members should consider their level of commitment to the ministry's mission, the amount of time they can commit to board activities, their level of comfort with fundraising efforts, their ability to make a sacrificial gift and provide access to their community of relationships, and their ability to abide by the ministry's conflict of interest policy.

YOU'RE ON THE BOARD: NOW WHAT?

A very important – and often overlooked – part of recruiting new board members is orientation and training. Let's face it, it can be awkward, confusing and downright inefficient to be thrown into your first board meeting without adequate training. On the other hand, an effective and well-planned orientation program can go a long way toward getting things off to a good start.

SUGGESTIONS FOR A BOARD
ORIENTATION PROGRAM

- Provide and discuss thoroughly an up-to-date board manual which would include:

    The organization's history and up-dated Constitution; bylaws; standing rules; policies and standards; organizational chart; most recent annual report; past year's board minutes; board calendar; personnel policies; past, present and projected financial budget; funding list; current and future program list and description; committee lists; board and staff directory, etc.

    A complete list of items that should be included in a board manual is contained in the Appendix.

- Provide a clearly written job description, outlining the duties and responsibilities of the new board member

- Arrange an introduction to and written profile of the other board members, including their background, tenure, special interests and skills relative to the organization

- Discuss board/staff relations, communication and interaction

- Describe time commitment – honestly

- Conduct a tour of the organization's facilities and operations with introductions to staff members

- Attend, by invitation, staff and committee meetings

- Discuss board committee structure

- Provide selected reading material related to the organization

Think of board member orientation as a process that may take three months or more. Initially, the new board member must receive enough information to be fully functional at the first board meeting. This may include the mission, vision and history of the organization, a board roster, recent meeting minutes and a list of current actions before the board. The board member should be assigned a "buddy" from the slate of experienced board members. This is the person the new board member can go to with questions or clarifications on board matters. Over the three-month period, the new board member thoroughly reviews the manual and can ask his or her buddy questions as they arise.

ONGOING BOARD TRAINING

Board training shouldn't end once your new board members are up to speed. Instead, board training and renewal should be a continuous process. Consider holding an annual board retreat or a series of dinner meetings to focus time and energy on planning and setting goals and priorities for the coming year. There is little time to undertake these long-range activities during normal business meetings, and a board retreat or series of longer dinner meetings ensures you will have adequate time to concentrate on these very important activities. The best time to do a planning retreat is within the first two months of a new board term and then annually thereafter.

Board members also should constantly seek out training opportunities in the areas related to their responsibilities: fundraising, including grant writing and grassroots fundraising; human resources; finance; and ethical and legal issues facing leadership boards. Just as staff members must hone their skills through training, so too must the leadership team. This can provide a tremendous boost to the organization.

ROLE OF THE BOARD OFFICERS

Each board of directors often includes the following officers: Board President (or Chairperson), Vice President (or Vice Chairperson), Secretary and Treasurer. These positions are normally elected annually, or, if there is a specified board term, each new board term. The following position descriptions are largely taken from BoardSource (http://www.boardsource.org), a resource for nonprofit boards.

The role of the Board Chairperson (or President) is to:

- Oversee board and Executive Committee meetings
- Serve as an ex-officio member of all committees
- Work in partnership with the Executive Director to make sure board resolutions are carried out
- Call special meetings if necessary
- Appoint all committee chairs and, with the Executive Director, recommend who will serve on committees
- Assist Executive Director in preparing agendas for board meetings
- Assist Executive Director in conducting new board member orientation
- Oversee searches for a new Executive Director
- Coordinate Executive Director's annual performance evaluation
- Work with the nominating committee to recruit new board members
- Act as an alternate spokesperson for the organization
- Periodically consult with board members on their roles and help them assess their performance

The role of the Vice Chairman (or Vice President) is to:

- Attend all board meetings
- Serve on the Executive Committee
- Carry out special assignments as requested by the Board Chair
- Understand the responsibilities of the Board Chairperson and be able to perform these duties in the Chairperson's absence
- Participate as a vital part of the board leadership
- In some organizations, the Board Vice Chairperson also serves as the Chair-Elect; in other words, the person who is in training to assume the role of Chairperson

The role of the Secretary is to:

- Attend all board meetings
- Serve on the Executive Committee
- Maintain all board records and ensure their accuracy and safety
- Review board minutes
- Assume responsibilities of the Chairperson in the absence of the Board Chairperson, Chair-Elect, and Vice Chairperson
- Provide notice of meetings of the board and/or of a committee when such notice is required

The role of the Treasurer is to:

- Attend all board meetings
- Understand financial accounting for nonprofit organizations
- Serve as financial officer of the organization and as Chairperson of the Finance Committee
- Manage, with the Finance Committee, the board's review of and action related to the board's financial responsibilities
- Work with the Executive Director and the Chief Financial Officer to ensure that appropriate financial reports are made available to the board on a timely basis
- Assist the Executive Director or the Chief Financial Officer in preparing the annual budget and presenting the budget to the board for approval
- Review the annual audit and answer board members' questions about the audit

ROLE OF THE BOARD CHAIRPERSON

As the chief volunteer officer, the Board Chairperson maintains a special role in the organization and operation of the board. Aside from fulfilling the role as defined above, the Board Chairperson must develop true leadership capability and inspire other board members to work as a team. Following the guidelines below will ensure your Board Chairperson gets off to a good start:

Know the job: Aside from on-the-job training, a good Board Chairperson will take every opportunity to improve his or her capability to do the job. The Chairperson may talk to other current and former Chairpeople about how to run a successful board. He or she may attend board training sessions or read up on the subjects of chairing a board, leadership and teamwork. Learning to run an effective meeting is a critical part of this board training. The Board Chairperson must learn how to write an agenda, stick to an agenda and operate a meeting efficiently. A sample agenda is included in the Appendix. The Board Chairperson also makes sure he or she knows the organization inside and out. To do this, he or she may talk to staff, volunteers and donors to learn about different programs and services.

Know your team: A major part of the Board Chairperson's role is to foster camaraderie with the Executive Director and among board members. The Board Chairperson should take the time to get to know the Executive Director, as well as fellow board members. This includes knowing their hopes, dreams and aspirations for the organization, why they became involved with the organization in the first place and what motivates them. In addition, a good Board Chairperson will seek opportunities to ensure everyone is heard during board meetings. If a board member has been noticeably silent on an issue, the Board Chairperson might say, "John, I don't think we've heard from you on this subject. What do you think about the proposal?" All of these efforts will ensure a more effective board over the long term.

Go out of your way: A good Board Chairperson will go out of the way to represent the nonprofit organization in the community. This means showing up to special events and important meetings in the community where the nonprofit should be represented. This may also include appearing on television, giving newspaper interviews, speaking to community groups and attending meetings with funders.

Look to the future: The Board Chairperson should also look to the future of the organization by developing future leadership. This includes identifying and mentoring potential board leaders. And, if the board does not have someone suitable to take over the Chairperson role at the end of the term, the current Board Chairperson will work to identify outside leadership.

BOARD COMMITTEES

Our earlier discussion about the role of Board Officers touched on the subject of Board Committees. The bottom line for larger boards is that committees often carry out most of the board work. These committees are composed of a mix of board members, staff and volunteers from the community. The committees meet regularly to work on tasks under their purview. They communicate to the board about their activities through committee reports submitted at each board meeting. And they discuss and make recommendations to the full board for approval or disapproval during regular board meetings.

Typically, there are two types of committees – standing and ad hoc. A standing committee is one that is in place all the time, for example the Finance Committee or the Executive Committee (we'll discuss these later). Standing committees are typically outlined in the nonprofit organization's bylaws. An ad hoc committee (also sometimes called a task force) is one created by the board for a limited, short-term purpose. For example, you may create an ad hoc committee to plan your 50th anniversary celebration or a one-time Homeless Summit. This committee would be disbanded once the activities are over.

Here are some traditional standing and ad hoc committees that you may see:

Executive Committee:
We discussed this important group earlier. This is the Executive Director's closest set of advisors. They make recommendations to the full board for approval. This group also acts for the full board on matters requiring immediate attention if it would be difficult to get the full board together either because the board is large or members are scattered about the country. The Executive Committee should not replace the full board; instead, the full board will typically approve any Executive Committee actions at the next full board meeting.

Board Development Committee:
Ensures effective board processes, structures and roles, including retreat planning, committee development, and board evaluation; sometimes includes roles of nominating committee, such as keeping a list of potential board members, and new member orientation and training.

Evaluation Committee:
Ensures sound evaluation of products/services/programs, including outcomes, goals, data, analysis and resulting adjustments.

Fundraising Committee (sometimes called the Finance Committee):
Oversees the organization's overall fundraising and, in particular, the fundraising done by the board. This includes working with staff to establish a fundraising plan. Note that the entire board is responsible for fundraising; the Fundraising Committee simply oversees this effort.

Finance Committee:
Reviews budgets, reports any financial irregularities, recommends financial guidelines, works with staff to draft financial reports, and works with the auditor unless there is a separate Audit Committee.

Program Committee:
Oversees program development, monitors existing programs, guides program evaluations, and helps establish program priorities.

Personnel Committee:
Drafts and revises personnel policies for board approval, reviews job descriptions, sets and reviews staff compensation levels, and leads review of chief executive.

Marketing/Public Relations Committee:
Represents the organization to the community; enhances the organization's image, including communications with the press; oversees development and implementation of marketing plan.

Nominating Committee:
Determines priorities for board composition, meets with prospective board members and recommends candidates to the full board, recommends a slate of officers, conducts orientation (along with staff) for new board members, suggests new, non-board members for committee members.

Audit Committee
Plans and supports audit of all major functions, e.g., finances, programs or organization.

Events Committee
Plans and coordinates major fundraising events, like a year-end banquet or concert; sometimes a subcommittee of the Fundraising Committee.

To be effective, each committee must have a committee job description and establish goals and objectives for each calendar year. We call this the Committee Terms of Reference. Once complete, the Terms of Reference document for each committee would be a part of the board manual.

ACTIVITY: COMMITTEE TERMS OF REFERENCE

Using the following Committee Terms of Reference sheet, complete a Committee Terms of Reference worksheet for one or more board committees. Choose your committee(s) from the list provided in the Board Committees section of this workbook.

COMMITTEE TERMS OF REFERENCE WORKSHEET

Name of Committee: _____

Date: _____ Planning Time frame (e.g., Jan–Dec 20XX) _____

Chairperson: _____

Committee Members: _____
_____
_____
_____

Report to Board: ❏ Monthly   ❏ Bi-monthly   ❏ Quarterly

Committee Outcome(s):
(What will be the end results or benefits of your committee's activities? What will your stakeholders have that they didn't have when you started?)

Committee Goals:
(Generally, how will your committee deliver the above outcome(s)? What will they do? What type of activities, events, initiatives, research, etc.? Note: these goals are fairly general and broad in nature and likely won't change much from year to year.)

Committee Objectives for the Upcoming Year:
(Specifically, what does this committee intend to accomplish? Use dates, specific numbers and dollars, defined projects and initiatives, etc.)

Immediate:
(Sell a certain number of tickets, write a volunteer position description, recruit a chairperson, draft a policy, etc.)

Medium:
(Produce a brochure, apply for a grant, conduct research, etc.)

Long term:
(Raise XX dollars, seek partnerships for concerts, etc.)

Budget Requirements:

CONCLUSION

As you can see, the board of directors plays a primary and important role in nonprofit organizations. They have vast responsibility, yet, unlike staff members, aren't paid for their work. A well-structured, well-managed and well-trained volunteer board is a must for ensuring nonprofit organizations carry out their mission and vision in the community.

In addition, an effective board ensures the future viability of the organization through fundraising and strategic planning activities. The following Appendices will provide you with the tools you need to build a better board.

GOD SPEED!

RESOURCES SHEET:

BoardSource (formerly the National Center for Nonprofit Boards) (www.boardsource.org)

Board Café: The newsletter for nonprofit boards (www.boardcafe.org)

Grassroots Fundraising Journal (www.grassrootsfundraising.org)

Charity Channel (www.charitychannel.com)

Chronicle of Philanthropy (www.philanthropy.com)

The Nonprofit Times (www.nptimes.com)

Internet Nonprofit Center (www.nonprofits.org)

QuickBooks Premier Nonprofit Edition (www.quickbooks.intuit.com)

The Vision Group, Ltd's ' "Grassroots Fundraising" Video Training
(www.getpublished.pro/products)

The Vision Group, Ltd's "Grant Writing and Fundraising for Christian Ministries"
Video Training
(www.getpublished.pro/products)

White Papers from The Vision Group, Ltd. - 30+ pages strictly on boards included with
the full training on How to Have the Most Effective Leadership Board on the Planet.
(www.getpublished.pro/products)

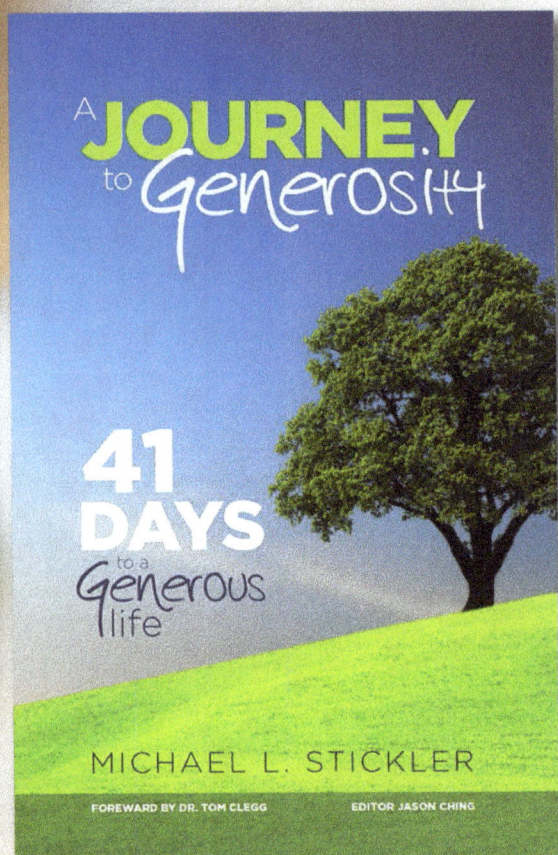

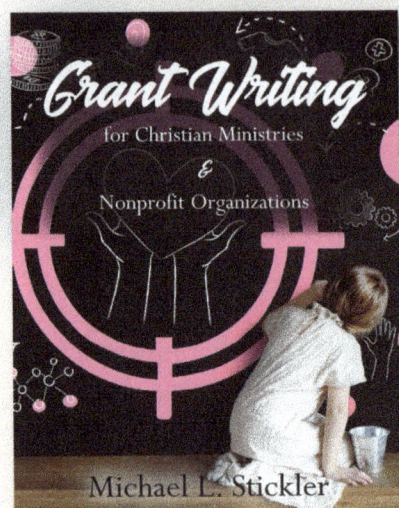

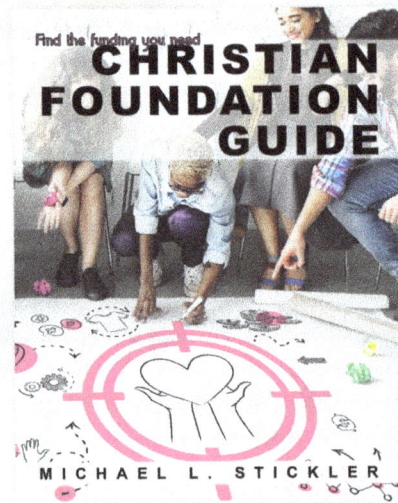

MICHAEL L. STICKLER

PUBLIC RELATIONS

NEWS · MEDIA · SOCIAL · MESSAGE · COMMUNICATION · SOCIETY · AUDIENCES · PUBLICITY · ADVERTISING · ORGANIZATION

FOR MINISTRY

MICHAEL L. STICKLER
WITH ARTHUR W. RITTER

Extreme
BOARD
Makeover

Your board meetings are a manifestation of effective leadership and governance. NOT the other way around.

MICHAEL L. STICKLER

GETTING OFF TO THE
RIGHT Start

CONTINUED
Success

VOLUNTEER
DEVELOPMENT

author
Michael L. Stickler

PROGRAM PLANNING
AND
EVALUATION

Projects

MICHAEL L. STICKLER

FOUNDATION
BUILDING
CAMPAIGN

Mike Stickler

Magnifying Your
Community Reach
The importance
of community relationships

MICHAEL L. STICKLER

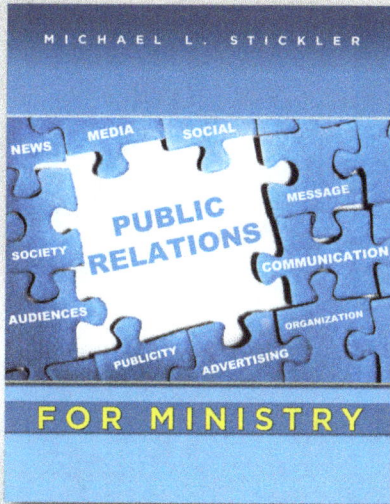

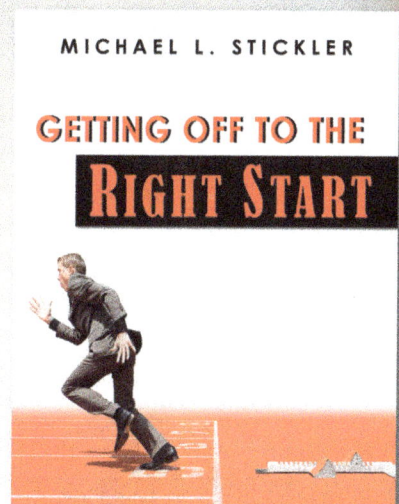

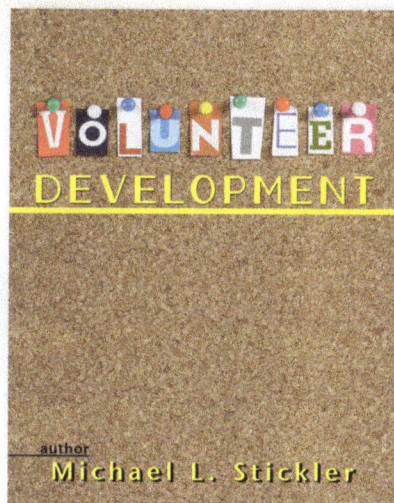

These resources and more @ **MikeStickler.online**

ISBN 978-0-9907441-7-7

51099

9 780990 744177

www.ingramcontent.com/pod-product-compliance
Lightning Source LLC
Chambersburg PA
CBHW080631030426
42336CB00018B/3160